OF WHICH
ANYTHING CONSISTS

❦

BARBARA MALOUTAS

OF WHICH
ANYTHING CONSISTS

BARBARA MALOUTAS

NEW MICHIGAN PRESS
TUCSON, ARIZONA

NEW MICHIGAN PRESS
DEPT OF ENGLISH, P. O. BOX 210067
UNIVERSITY OF ARIZONA
TUCSON, AZ 85721-0067

<http://newmichiganpress.com/nmp>

Orders and queries to nmp@thediagram.com.

Copyright © 2011 by Barbara Maloutas.
All rights reserved.

ISBN 978-1-934832-32-5. FIRST PRINTING.

Printed in the United States of America.

Design by Ander Monson.

Cover photos by Barbara Maloutas. Top and bottom: Santa Monica Beach and Pier during Santa Monica Glow Festival; Middle: iced tree trunk stump in Hessel Park, Champaign IL; Background for title: parking lot on Antelope Island State Park within the Great Salt Lake; Back cover: "The *Bean*," Millennium Park's *Cloud Gate* sculpture by Anish Kapoor in Chicago.

CONTENTS

1

WATER	1
FIRE	2
EARTH	3
AIR	4

2

WATER	7
FIRE	8
EARTH	9
AIR	10

3

WATER	13
FIRE	14
EARTH	15
AIR	16

4

WATER	19
FIRE	20
EARTH	21
AIR	22

5

WATER	25
FIRE	26
EARTH	27
AIR	28

6

WATER	31
FIRE	32
EARTH	33
AIR	34

7

WATER	37
FIRE	38
EARTH	39
AIR	40

8

WATER	43
FIRE	44
EARTH	45
AIR	46

Acknowledgments   49

1

WATER

what water; what water is missing; and when; before everything; there was never enough water; this island; water surrounds—they say sea; they—aware of—scarcity and all methods of keeping; islanders with water; in water; of water

writing from memory without concern—of structure; this thinking of cisterns—a reservoir—with less than ever; concern for story; never knowing

enough but—remember how easily a low green tanker; just out of sea; water-full-heavy; full—objects of; greater density than—are floating; can; hooked up to a reservoir; pumping at night; in time to harbor; to release

this not knowing is made; membering; a low boat in water—in harbor; the possibility there's some other—harbor not this one; asking the difference; bare hand; no gloves or a bucket; in hand; so measured—take water; short showers; tight water; a commodity—in memory; in memoriam; a reservoir

1

FIRE

when a house is on fire; prevent by closing—all air currents; I want a fire—in the case of a house; to smother die out be done; check the doors; preserve time to get help; not to consider the terror of—bars; to brand some neighborhoods dangerous

if upstairs; tear off your clothing; make cords; to let yourself down by; no shame in; this nakedness—is necessary; but furniture is not—an issue; let it burn

above all crawl—like a snake when—a room is filled; stay calm; or on fire; it is colder on a floor; proven more free; than fire

1

EARTH

always in bloom for January one; earthnuts; or tubers—at least; gypsies collect them; along roads; sell them in the city; cupped—moist in tin-foil; trays of earthnuts—they're lucky and handily displayed; for luck—earth-tucked umbels

people within a people; festival bracelets of florescence—sell cheaply on saints days; and patent shoe feasts—hands swaying; skirted hips—without shame

seen—seem smiling; keepers of beginnings and endings; their once—twice smiling faces to gate-keep—each; in one direction; sometimes—we are deceived; to believe what is false; disbelieve what is true

we carry a first song; through

1

AIR

how it takes; air; we sit in it—the air; we breathe in; in—animal animate anima; and out again; how we breathe—ourselves alive; it is skin around us; it—not us; it breathes and bellows; we in it; and out now

and if air is acted on; in the rising of warm air; sun acts; acts on air—warm air; swoops towards cool—evening; for evening cool; there is only so much—air; as a pie is divided; one piece at a time; a bit of fresh air

the tumble of—wind; the amount is constant; or perhaps not—the question; we can't see wind—but evidence of; and temperatures vary; constant describes air scientifically; in motion constantly; it's the old wind in the willows—the only sound of it; forecasting winds tonight—called relentless

2

WATER

there is a story that is clear

as water to a teller—who writes the story; she writes; she makes a beach—of summer; moving and up the Atlantic coast; down the shore; Jersey white cap and all; over her right shoulder—since; she swims north on her back; better to float; and a family—under one wide umbrella; large-orange and green-striped; she is proud of lone stroking—her cap; one-piece suit

at times; in time we see; have seen various—small insects skate across water; the surface; acknowledge that; extremely thin membrane

while a felt or silk hat; held so as to keep a crown full of air; sustains well; a person above water—a great length of time; a drowning body bloated; all those who have drowned; writers too

2

FIRE

a destroyer is; many a destructive; fires originate in carelessness; in handling ashes; there are improper; places and wooden receptacles; it seems almost; spontaneous; with a sieve—a metal container can—catch unburned coals; the ashes pass and to remember dust

half the pleasure of an open fire; is open; rather than upward; when sparks fly; guards do not—shut out heat or affect a draft; a carpet that's on fire; materially—first always—put out a fire; that's on fire

if nothing else—is at hand; throw a burning person on the floor; wrapped in a carpet or rug; your coat—if nothing else; we know

the know how in emergency; and fire

2

EARTH

a woman crosses a border; she wears a winter cape; it is summer; below her cape—an inside child; chthonian—without expecting an initial ch—dwelling in; or beneath the surface of earth

along streets—long gypsy skirts; sitting—to hold babies—sleeping; lap babies; *metera's* outstretched—only one hand; and head-tilt; feigned reticence; *parakalo*—don't look—if you don't; wanting to give

in our new year; their children ringing triangles—sing-song; I can hum it on the first; when was it—first; good gypsy music

shooed from cafés; in a square called—little column—*kolonaki*; shooed birds; speaking a language of children without children; our watching them and distance kept; a bilking

umbelliferous beneath; a little umbel; and thus caped

2

AIR

as canaries; as birds—do not keep them; do not room; a room being painted; has an odor of new paint; no birds in new paint; like mining birds in mines; yellow birds; a bird warning—of bad air

do not; likewise; the wisdom of like; set a cage in a window; the point; the wisdom; use a cage or head cover; a draft is injurious; like injury air

birds; do not keep birds; for a start as dental in *thē-a*; as aunt in the end; so write—*thē-a An-a-sta-see-a*; *Anastasia* keeps birds in cages; swinging cages from a ceiling; lots of birds; *thē-o*; Costa in bed; uncle collector; of taxes—and birds; below—their chirping; it was *thē-o*; who together kept birds; ill with fever

if you intend to breed; birds—say in spring; do not cage—in winter together; during winter birds don't even breed; won't is a question; single birds kept in a room—as birds breeding; or males and females in mating season— similar; in the same room; like *thē-o* and *thē-a* in bed; in separate—cages; causing mating—fever

3

WATER

to keep ice-water; icy; make a hat-shaped cover of two thicknesses; strong brown paper; with—was it—it was; before our time; cotton batting quilted; between old practices—as thermos; large enough to drop over—completely envelop a pitcher; this works; prevents warm air from coming; in contact with pitcher

 iced water; ice from ice-houses; cut to carry; frigid water; not women—perhaps; the shape of a pitcher; some pitchers and women; ice floats and ice beds; wishing for anti-freeze; his glacier; allowing it to melt; send regards to Weiner

 once I drank it; the opposite of anti-freeze; not pop; not really dying; from drinking—a can; ice-lasting; a long—long time

3

FIRE

once he held fire in him; now someone's against him; homeless he; we; they find him; he's burning; burning—up

    splashing fuel; a blaze; no way to escape it; a fiery—no flight; getting away with it; without any apparent; provocation

    a usual corner; of a world; the world; imagine the fuel—for any night—alive—live a live; oh

    a homeless Ambassador; a bell-hop; hot foots it—I wish; they say he had had; a neighborly orbit

    cry uncle; Uncle Johnny—his obit; fire

3

EARTH

where we stand—a day; dirt is stone; stone is dirt; soil resembling parent rock—at first; in time—it becomes impossible—to tell; and if all soils—slowly get deeper and deeper; dirt turns to soil; a small bit—of life: soil lives

why half of soil is holes as; ants rodents earthworms—till it; tilling—not to waste their deaths; 100,000 earthworms—in our one backyard; air in soil moist with—CO_2—leaks from soil exchange; so that

dirt is clay; clay is negative—takes to positive; living thrives with neutral

all rock is crystal and—

earth barely exists

3

AIR

holding a candle; up—higher than the mouth; in blowing it out; into darkness; out—can't hold a candle; dispossess—ing—in huffing and puffing; to blow it out; with an upward instead of; downward—current

in blowing out a candle; ill omen—if a candle goes out; to blow one out; if what is wicked; to keep anger smoldering; thus to be blown out; the air; the wick not the wicked will; not smolder down

we out and not wicked; wolf—hold a candle; thus *b* has a puff sound as in big or bad; the *d* of down and end; where the teeth and tongue; in stop that—doesn't help

WATER

hanging; death has the same cause as drowning; it says it; not me; cut down the body without allowing it to fall; place a body face down; pressing the back of a tongue with a finger—if you can; to allow any accumulation; it escapes—really they say it says; lay on body back now; treat as directed; they say—place; drowned writers

    example; for a body still warm; after removal of clothing; stand off six feet; dash several times; a bowl of cold water—to face neck and chest; to revive use—icy water; for a body still; warm

4

FIRE

for burns—equal parts of lime water; and raw—linseed oil; writing to herself; her family house is gone; a palimpsest of burning; burned down; her fiery hair is fire red

    injury to the lungs; cf exposing the neck and face; prevent breathing hot air; then injury to the lungs call; a doctor then as now

    wait—a superficial burn; covering a large surface; is most relative; to surface; a deeper one confined to less; surface; surface is not; as dangerous—only in a case of fire

    a water dressing of two or more; thicknesses of old linen; this plucky housewife—and old; linen a little larger than a wound

    sticking plaster sticks; apply water to keep it wet; a confluence of water and skin on fire

4

EARTH

I write a note; don't expect my daughter; not deliverable; earth has quaked; full earth-shock; at least one violent oscillation—a continuance; the numbers; seven point four; at sixes and sevens; at *Rond Pointe de Paradis* 6—Latin sex; Greek sounds like—exy

Genesis 6—"the whole earth was—of one language"

a mass of six sextillions of tons; the faulting of rocks; the faulting of a guest who moves in; uninvited; with sickly child

where'd they come from; this extreme; never thought to say no; their own supplies; own food; own radio; their own—own; as whose property is this; in my house; my life is stored and here storied; what right in an—*apothiki*—a storehouse of things; to live; now survive this quake

4

AIR

prevailing but; virtue—not always—prevailing for naught; those westerlies; blowing across and prevailing; chaos between thirty and sixty; degrees how; he says for chaos—as in house or south—*chouse*; the earth's rotation deflects; cause and; effects—prevailing westerlies

    there are fronts of pressure; there is no f—in the roots of indo-european; look long and hard; through air—how the tangle becomes clear; the pressure of heavy derivatives; specifically when aus- is; as east easter aurora; westerlies are somehow; opposite to light; their opposite—barely a morning; so that in dark dawn; dances—air carried; guessing *borealis*—finding every day

5

WATER

continue—if poison; if possible with copious draughts of water; warm water; till—not until—the poison is entirely; removed by water; a flushing; think about the uses of flushing; to yourself

no longer considered a mark of high mind; type of mind; to faint away; this feminine at the smallest fright; not to sink into helplessness; at first sign—the appearance of danger; evidence of a clear brain; at once; self-possession in a pinch; emergency

at a critical moment; besides; fright and confusion are a confession; as ignorance; as well as; want of much self-control

learning what to do as a guide; is to read without practice

5

FIRE

a dressing of pure hog's lard is best; boil till it settles and then; floating lard hardens; keeping out the air

    white of an egg—works

    shaving lather—works

    common cooking soda used for—works; we don't know; any longer what exactly; works or why

    forgetting is desired; or is forgetting so—not fire

5

EARTH

a father's tumescent masculinity; he has them; *bollix*—comes from old English—*beallucas*—testicles; there—a more familiar word; less complicating

he bargains; insures insurance; for families with dependent children; a wife pregnant; so a father goes straight to an answer; to a city like—Sacramento—outward sign of inward grace; his wife with child; umbelliferous

I once studied a catechism with gloves on; now rare—as *bollix*; he is porous—he knows no borders; has *beallucas*; what is more earth—then?

5

AIR

to clean wells of foul air; take a peck of—unslaked lime; throw it down—a well; but watch out; there is combustion; an action reaction occurs—is carried out; and with it; foul air; cf—is comes from; all possible old roots

    un-slaked should be listed; as a common—a chemical reaction; not made less intense; by satisfying as desire; to go in or out with a rush; experience it for yourself; a little peck; when it's more than enough

    this ending of foul air; this whoosh—from a well

6

WATER

the *i*-sound in sin and; sieve with a same short sound; I have always thought my mother short; not I; holding water in one's hand—the best one can do is; take a sip—before it is gone

witches were tested by water—this no-win never situation; or is this another wish; likely lie; I never knew—Salem abbreviates Jerusalem; in 1692—as well; founding fathers

suspicion falls; falls on; from interest in science—in investigation; thinking of child-wonder at simple surface tension; thus a drop of water tends—to assume the shape of a sphere; to act like

is this before or after the testing; for Jeru Salem; when like attracts like; and if one is unlike; what then about such; seeping—such; as in capillary action and boarding; water

6

FIRE

"vapours from whose solid atmosphere; black rain—and fire; and hail will burst"; an ode and this to west wind

    and when dousing of an inward fire—possessed; a quiet digestion against a stomach's fire; this tell-tale at least; life's rush to overtake; imagination

    so doused and falls on stone—oh slippery; flagstone—its hollow sound; and to what degree in writing fire; language like a firebrand; to douse it not—a stick; flaming in the hand; the slippage that conjures—two thrums and then a twang; expecting water; work the twang; thus blow on fire

6

EARTH

oh, Siphnos; island earth

    one single room; to live and pot in—at once; light of orange-red; an earthen mound off; to the side—of clay; printed sundress of a potter's wife; stained all red; from earth not blood; she misses two teeth and cooks there as—well

    cooled water in jugs in the back-of-a-chapel—a room; we rented a week; a chapel in honor of the child they never had; each spring with lime; slapped white; as well—our stunned eyes

    we still use it; his earthenware dish packed in my clothes; my own kids; playing with neighbors' chickens; island neighbors—that is; why were they without clothes; were they sweet in our obsession; with sweetness as new white; their white bottoms

6

AIR

charcoal acts on air; it sweetens it; sweet exchange an easy change

for offensive air in apartments; place charcoal—on trays in a suite of rooms; "lying in wait is not writing"; it is so—very porous; it absorbs—condenses gases; there are promises they used to offer; one cubic inch of fresh—charcoal absorbs; one hundred inches of some gases away; to qualify—neither which nor all; just exchange of air; just some; gases full with bad air—no analysis; simple practice

better yet; imagine it; strewn over heaps—of decomposing pelts; and over dead animals; even with a contradiction in animals meaning animate; but for the dead—charcoal prevents unpleasant odors; acting on changes; and permeable by air; and pours—porous; over my dead—who knows

"the wide earth...and coalesced in all its various parts..."; reading coal in coalesced; writing its sweetness

7

WATER

how lonely she looks in water—she a part of it; is a body of water; it is as if—she; alone is a body of water; she is water; she looks under water and—does not see
   her murkiness

7

FIRE

steaming is safer; than either boiling or baking; all requiring fire; the pudding should be; as a result light—and wholesome; a quality of fire

then there's grandma; Thompson's white pudding; made with suet; always perfectly sweet; formed from best ingredients; in equal parts with shifted flour; season "very highly"—say with pepper; "stuff loosely in beef entrails"; is this then earth—or fire; must should must and then—there's entrails at the heart; its darkness

the above was considered an "extra" dish; at most all them "flax scutchings"—so as; one way to put out fire; to dress cf—from beating; "quilting frolics" and "log rollings"—say one hundred years ago; both sweet and peppery—one's stomach is on fire

EARTH

we exclude earth from our thoughts; refuse to—consider its huge—its rough enormity; filled "of wilds and dark mottling"—when solitude is one hand in a forest; a wild—monstrous giant to dwarf and crush

    not one heritage tomato grew this summer; I scrape the surface—merely; know only of its traffic; nothing of its depths

    fruitful and multiply—fill the earth and subdue it; why it's our liquid amber trees tamed and trimmed; the giant is still there; and will he; Wally—thank you

7

AIR

Norse madman—old *Odin*; somehow folksy; rages by means of wind; spirit of driven—air; leaves tremble—and so we; yet to free grain from its chaff using air

and still flutter in French; ankle wings—so demure; a *Mercredi*—messenger; we do not shoot—the pleasure; a carrier pigeon carries no weight; a message

and if a man grow old; wooden in his ways; *Wodin*—really a prophet—the dead attend; tend him—them; if he runs that far; until death do

and what of *Wodin's* day; pissed his name has come to this to Wednesday; cf—comes from; even wisdom—even I; even *Icarus*; there is no fire without air

WATER

and do you remember that the daughters of Danaos; were all; all condemned to collect water with a sieve

there is none or little hope; to dampen the flames of their hell with; fewer than a few drops

and of the one daughter who did not do-in her bridegroom—she-bride—why I wonder; what empathy saved her; and in consequence; her-him

a daughter not attached to her father; to attach herself to—what's new; perhaps; family; and whither thou

withering

8

FIRE

poor wretch; whose corpse they burnt with fire; upon a purple-covered—spice strewn pyre; a firestorm—an ethical—concern; in death that is a birth

despite evidence; oblivious—these fat cats; short on shame; our vanities; all blowing off; a risk in bonfires; of collapse; the least to say; and said

but I'm not done; not now—at last; to add an *e* and so at least; there is a heart and theirs; of rapture—and of fire

8

EARTH

three year; Code of Hammurabi—1792 B.C.; use it or lose it; the essence of possession

    love of dirt is passion—as is the latest; while mudpies satisfy; our best instinct to be dirty—we are pure; fondness for the ground returns after life; better—living; eating dirt; running round; sewing oats; a world wind—of all the mud there is

    smelling like dirt in spring; love of digging in the ground; surely; as sure to come back as—surely to go under ground; to stay there

    details are all there are; and the earth is dunged

8

AIR

"...the poison that replaces air took over"; cf—(G)ood luck

Louise and windmills

two people; too long; together—banter conspiracy theories on the wind; decay goes on somewhere

pure air enters the lungs—becomes charged with waste particles; poison if taken back again; an adult spoils one gallon of pure air every minute; or twenty-five flour—barrelfuls; that's a single night; think of these facts beforehand; before nailing down windows for the winter; not in—but for—winter

ACKNOWLEDGMENTS

"A Reason of Water, 1-8," *Octopus Magazine* #11; "A Reason of Air, 1-8," *Kadar Koli* 5; "A Reason of Earth," *Luvina* 57.

Pie in the Sky Press printed a fine press limited edition of the poems from the water series, entitled *a reason of water*.

COLOPHON

Text is set in a digital version of Jenson, designed by Robert Slimbach in 1996, and based on the work of punchcutter, printer, and publisher Nicolas Jenson.

BARBARA MALOUTAS is the 2008 Sawtooth Poetry Prize winner for *the whole Marie*, (Ahsahta Press). Her previous book and chapbooks are *In a Combination of Practices* (New Issues Press), *Coffee Hazilly* (Beard of Bees) and *Practices* (New Michigan Press). In 2010 Les Figues Press published online *Her Not Blessed*, a response to Harold Abramowitz's *Not Blessed*. Pie in the Sky Press published a limited fine press edition of the water series from *of which anything consists*. Her work has appeared or is forthcoming in journals including *Aufgabe, Free Verse, Segue, Tarpaulin Sky, Good Foot, The New Review of Literature, bird dog, dusie, elimae, Interbirth Books, Greatcoat, OR, Puerto del Sol, kadar koli, Octopus,* and *Luvina*.

NEW MICHIGAN PRESS, based in Tucson, Arizona, prints poetry and prose chapbooks, especially work that transcends traditional genre. Together with DIAGRAM, NMP sponsors a yearly chapbook competition.

DIAGRAM, a journal of text, art, and schematic, is published bimonthly at THEDIAGRAM.COM. Periodic print anthologies are available from the New Michigan Press at NEWMICHIGANPRESS.COM/NMP.